Willow

The Highly Sensitive Pup

Written by
Mandy Mayock, MA, LPC

Illustrated by
Tammie Lyon

Copyright © 2022 by Amanda Mayock
Illustrated by Tammie Lyon

All rights reserved. No part of this publication may be reproduced, distributed, or transmitted in any form or by any means, including photocopying, recording, or other electronic or mechanical methods, without the prior written permission of the publisher, except in the case of brief quotations embodied in reviews and specific other non-commercial uses permitted by copyright law.

This book is a work of fiction.
Names, characters, places, and incidents are either the product of the author's imagination or are used fictitiously. Any resemblance to actual persons, living or dead, events, or locales is entirely coincidental.

Printed in the United States of America

Paperback ISBN: 978-1-956019-62-9
Hardcover ISBN: 978-1-956019-61-2
eBook ISBN: 978-1-956019-63-6

Library of Congress Control Number: 2022945399

Published by DartFrog Plus,
the hybrid publishing imprint of DartFrog Books.

DartFrog Books
4697 Main Street
Manchester, VT 05255
www.DartFrogBooks.com

*For Mackenzie and Jack
and all the rescue puppies*

A portion of the proceeds of this book will be donated to support The Sato Project

I am a very lucky dog. I was given a second chance before I was even born. My mother was living alone on a beach in Puerto Rico when The Sato Project rescued her.

Sato means "street dog", but I am not a street dog. I was born in a veterinarian's office and together with my mother, brothers and sisters, we flew from Puerto Rico to New York City to be adopted!

From the beginning, the volunteers could tell I was not like the other dogs, but even though I was a little different, a family came along and chose me because they knew I was special.

My new family named me Willow because I am gentle and sweet like a beautiful willow tree. Little did they know that my differences also gave me superpowers!

My superpowers don't look like "traditional" superpowers.

I can't fly or see through walls, but they are still cool—maybe even cooler.

I have a super-brain, and I think about everything...A LOT. I have SO many thoughts inside my head all the time! Sometimes I wonder, *How do I choose just one thing to think about?*

I have super eyesight; they wonder why I don't like bright lights, inside or out.

I have super hearing; my new family wonders why loud noises scare me.

I have super feelings; I get upset when I'm told I am doing something wrong, even though I know my humans are just trying to help me.

My body is super sensitive; they wonder why I don't like scratchy things or when my collar is too tight, too loose, or just itchy!

I also get upset when I feel like I have too much to do.

Sit, stay, stop, let's

But when I get upset, about whatever, I go to my room or another quiet place and take a break.

ay ball, FETCH, drop it, GOOD GIRL!

One day, during a visit to the veterinarian, my family learned what makes me unique. I am an HSP, or a highly sensitive pup. That is my superpower!

Being a highly sensitive pup means I am hyperaware of everything (and everyone) around me. I'm always on alert, watching and listening.

I have super feelings, sometimes, when I see something beautiful, I feel like I may cry.

I can also sense when others are not ok. I love to comfort them and make them feel better.

But my very best superpower is that I have a huge heart and love very, very deeply, whether it is my family, my friends, or my squeaky toy.

It turns out that being highly sensitive is supercool... except for not liking loud noises, bright lights, or itchy clothing. THAT'S kind of annoying.

I am not the only one with highly sensitive superpowers. There are many of us and not just puppies. Maybe YOU are a highly sensitive person too.

In fact, one in every five people in the world is a highly sensitive person. They may be your friends, someone in your family, your teacher, or maybe even your doctor or delivery person. Even some movie stars are highly sensitive people!

So, now that you know about highly sensitive people, you should know that...

It's **OK** to be sensitive.

It's **OK** to have strong feelings.

It's **OK** if you need to take a break and be quiet sometimes.

When I take a break, I like to be alone, rest, and breathe deeply with my eyes closed. But a break can be whatever helps YOU feel calmer. Maybe you prefer to go for a walk, draw, play with a specific toy, or look at your favorite book.

It's more than ok to be a highly sensitive person. It's awesome!

YOU are awesome!

YOU are a superhero!

I believe in YOU!

For Parents and Caregivers

Have you noticed your child displaying some of Willow's highly sensitive characteristics?

- Strong reactions to both external and internal stimuli
- Overwhelmed by loud noises, bright lights, and strong smells
- Sensitive to pain, stress, and hunger
- Bothered by the clothing they consider itchy, too tight, or uncomfortable
- Cautious (anxious) in new situations
- Struggles with change
- Keenly aware of changes in their environment and people's moods
- Detail-oriented
- Introspective, quiet, or a deep thinker
- Increased emotional sensitivity
- Inquisitive with self and others/reflective
- Intuitive or perceptive
- Highly empathetic
- Creative

A highly sensitive person (or HSP) has a specific collection of personality traits. It is not a clinical diagnosis. It is a term that psychologist Elaine Aron created in 1996. There is no scientific test a child can take to measure how sensitive they are, but there is an online assessment you can fill out at www.hsperson.com to help determine if a child has these traits.

Highly sensitive children are often mischaracterized as shy, anxious, or awkward. Identifying a child as an HSP or identifying their HSP tendencies helps you and others understand their emotional reactions and behaviors. It also gives you context that will help you support them. It is not a "label" or a "problem," but simply helpful information.

As with any personality type, being a highly sensitive person has its pros and cons. Having big feelings is hard to manage at any age, but here are some ways you can support the highly sensitive person in your life.

1. Acceptance: This personality type is formed through genetics and environmental factors. They

were born this way and look to you for love and acceptance. Your unconditional support will enable them to feel more comfortable and confident.

2. Communication: Help your child label their feelings, whether good or bad. Putting feelings into words helps children understand them and demonstrate self-control—model sharing your feelings and encourage your child to do the same.

3. Identify your child's triggers: Each child has their sensitivities. Once you understand what affects them, you can work together to avoid or learn to cope with these situations.

4. The importance of downtime: HSP children may need more rest to unwind, recover, and recharge after being out in the world. Being mindful of their schedules and not planning back-to-back events helps keep them from feeling overwhelmed. HSPs have been known to go out of their way to avoid overwhelming situations for fear of being emotionally flooded.

5. **Use your words kindly:** When you need to discipline or correct your child, it is more effective to use gentle reminders than harsh words. HSPs generally shut down when confronted and can take a long time to recover.

6. **Try to stay calm and consistent:** As with all parenting methods, modeling appropriate behavior (including your own self-care) and being consistent helps with your child's emotional wellbeing. HSP children benefit from clear and direct communication.

7. **Superpower:** Celebrate your child's superpower! Highlight their strengths. Where does your child excel? There are so many beautiful gifts they have because they are a highly sensitive person.

There is no "treatment" for high sensitivity, but with self-knowledge, self-care, and healthy boundaries, an individual with HSP can live a wonderfully full and rich life. For more information on HSP adults and children, please check out any of Elaine Aron's books on the subject and www.hsperson.com.

Fun fact!

Evolutionary research has found this trait in more than 100 nonhuman species, including dogs and cats.

About the Author

Mandy Mayock, MA, LPC spends her time between Wayne, Pennsylvania, Ocean City, New Jersey and St. Simons Island, Georgia. She lives with her husband Mike and her totally spoiled rescue dogs: Willow, a Sato from Puerto Rico, and Peter, a Jack Russell/Chihuahua who was rescued from a kill shelter in Tennessee.

She received her undergraduate education from the University of Toronto and completed her Master's degree in counseling at Eastern University. She is an active member of the American Counseling Association and is licensed in Pennsylvania and Nevada. She has four children - Mackenzie, Jack, Leigh and Michael. She is a member of the Society of Children's Book Writers and Illustrators and is in the process of writing another book featuring Willow's brother Pete, while she studies to become an oyster farmer.

You can follow Willow and Pete's adventures on their instagram @willowandpetemayock

About the Illustrator

Tammie Lyon lives in Cincinnati, Ohio with her husband Lee and their two rescue dogs, Amos and Artie.

Tammie has a BFA from Columbus College of Art and Design and is an award winning author and illustrator. She has illustrated work for Disney, Scholastic, Simon and Schuster, Penguin, Harper Collins and Amazon Publishing to name a few. She is also an author of her own stories. Her first picture book, Olive and Snowflake, was released to starred reviews from Kirkus and School Library Journal. She spends her days in her studio in the woods surrounded by wildlife and, of course, two mostly-always-sleeping dogs.

THE SATO PROJECT

The Sato Project is dedicated to rescuing abused and abandoned dogs in Puerto Rico, where an estimated 500,000 stray dogs are roaming the island. One dog at a time, they are saving lives, fighting back, and building permanent change. Sato is a local Puerto Rican term for a mixed-breed, stray dog. In its first 10 years, The Sato Project rescued over 6,000 satos, rehabilitated them with the highest standards of veterinary care, and placed them in loving homes in the mainland U.S. They also address the underlying causes of overpopulation, abandonment, and abuse through community outreach and low or no-cost spay/neuter and vaccination programs. After the devastation of Hurricane Maria in 2017, the earthquakes of 2020, and the COVID-19 pandemic, The Sato Project also expanded into disaster relief efforts: distributing humanitarian and animal emergency supplies, pulling dogs from overburdened municipal shelters with over 94% euthanasia rates, and reuniting families with their beloved pets.

Learn more about The Sato Project at thesatoproject.org.

Printed in the USA
CPSIA information can be obtained
at www.ICGtesting.com
LVHW070516131124
796448LV00002B/2